Boxing The Dent Out Of Literacy

Written by Yvette Gittens

Early Childhood Practitioner and Literacy Specialist

Dedicated to my sons and to all the parents, teachers and students who may use this Pre-primer and Primer reader.

Kindergarten to Grade 2 levels (4-7 years old)

Motto: Read, Share and Grow Together

Illustration Acknowledgements

Public Domain Images: These are images to which no exclusive intellectual property rights apply. These rights have expired, been forfeited or are inapplicable.

Creative Commons Licensed Images: These are public copyright licenses that enable the free distribution of copyrighted work to be used, and modified, as long as the work is attributed by the author.

All rights reserved.

No part of this book may be reproduced in any form by photocopying or any electronic or mechanical means, including information storage or retrieval systems, without permissions in writing from both the copyright owner and the publisher of the book.

First published 2022

© Yvette Gittens 2022

Cover Designed by: Yvette Gittens

ISBN: 9798366524827

| Aa | Letter a for apple

I am an Apple

I am an apple.

apple apple apple

I can be red.

I can be green.

Read and Recall:

am an red green be can

Bb Letter b for bat

I See a Bat

I see a bat.

bat bat bat

Bet bats the ball,

over the wall.

Read and Recall:

see **the** **over**

Cc Letter c for cat

I See a Cat

I see a cat.

cat cat cat

I see a big, fat cat.

Sam is my brown, fat cat.

I like my big, fat cat Sam.

Read and Recall:

big is my like brown

Dd Letter d for dog

The Dog is Jet

I see a dog.

dog dog dog

The dog is Jet.

Jet is at the vet.

Jet is not well.

Read and Recall:

see is at the not well

Ee Letter e for egg

I am an Egg

I am an egg.

egg   egg   egg

The hen lays an egg.

The egg is in the pan.

Read and Recall:

am   an   the   lays   is   in

Ff Letter f for fish

The Red Fish

I see a fish.

fish fish fish

I see a red fish on a dish.

Read and Recall:

see   the   red   on

Gg Letter g for goat

Gus The Goat

Gus the goat is my pet.

goat goat goat

Gus likes to eat grass.

Gus likes green grass.

Read and Recall:

the is my likes to green

Hh Letter h for hen

The Red Hen

I see the red hen.

hen hen hen

The hen lays an egg.

The hen is happy.

Read and Recall:

the see lays an is happy

| Ii | Letter i for ink

The Black Ink

I write with a black ink.

ink   ink   ink

Black ink looks like night.

Read and Recall:

write   black   looks   like   night

Jj Letter j for jug

The Juice Jug

I see the juice jug.

jug   jug   jug

Juice is in the jug.

Read and Recall:

the   see   in   juice

Kk Letter k for kite

Kip and His Kite

Kip has a kite.

kite   kite   kite

Kip can fly his kite.

His kite is red.

Read and Recall:

and   his   can   fly   has   red

| Ll | Letter L for legs

My Two Legs

I see one leg. I see two legs.

leg legs leg legs

My two legs can make me walk.

Read and Recall:

my one two can make me

Mm Letter m for mat

Molly The Cat

I see a cat.

The cat is on the mat.

mat mat mat

The cat likes to sleep.

It is Molly the cat.

Read and Recall:

the see it on likes to sleep

Nn Letter n for net

Jet and The Net

I see a net.

net net net

The man runs after

Jet, with his net.

Read and Recall:

his the see runs after with

| Oo | Letter o for ox |

Oxmo The Ox

Oxmo is an ox.

ox ox ox

Oxmo is a big ox.

He has two horns.

Read and Recall:

big   he   has   two   horns

| Pp | Letter p for pet

Jet The Pet

Jet is my pet.

pet pet pet

Jet is a happy pet.

Read and Recall:

is my happy

Qq Letter q for queen

The Happy Queen

I see the queen.

queen queen queen

The queen has a

crown on her head.

The queen looks happy.

Read and Recall:

see crown her head happy

| Rr | Letter r for red

The Red Kite

I see red.

red red red

Ted has a red kite.

Read and Recall:

the see has red

Ss | Letter s for sun

The Hot Sun

The sun is hot.

sun sun sun

The sun is very hot

Read and Recall:

the is hot very

Tt Letter t for toys

The Toy Truck

Ted likes to play.

Ted is in my toy truck.

toy toy toy

Ted is happy.

Read and Recall:

play my to happy in

Uu Letter u for umbrella

Under The Umbrella

The rain is coming.

umbrella umbrella

Kim is under the

umbrella.

Read and Recall:

the is coming under

Vv Letter v for van

The Big Red Van

Here comes the big red van.

van van van

Sam is in the van.

Read and Recall:

here comes the big in

Ww Letter w for web

The Spider's Web

Jeb saw a spider in the web.

web web web

The spider's home is a web.

Read and Recall:

saw   the   home   in

Xx Letter x for x-ray

X is for X-ray

X is for x-ray.

X-ray x-ray x-ray

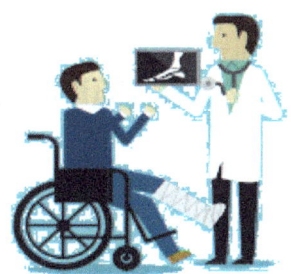

I can see the inside of my leg, under an x-ray.

Read and Recall:

for can see my under an

Yy Letter y for yam

The Brown Yam

The brown yam is big.

yam yam yam

I like to eat yam pie.

Read and Recall:

brown is like to eat pie

Zz Letter z for zip

I Can Zip

Mom look! I can zip my pants.

zip zip zip

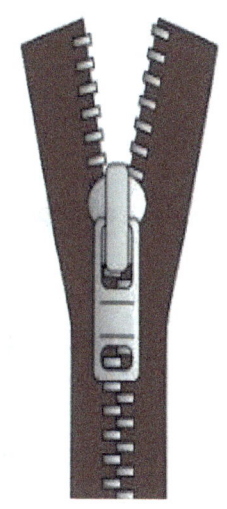

I go up, up, up.

I can zip.

Read and Recall:

look can my go up can

| ab |

Word Family

ab
The Cab

I see a cab.

The cab is red.

The cab will take me to school.

Read and Recall:

see the will take me to

| ad | Word Family

ad
🟢

<u>My Dad</u>

My dad is the best dad.

I am glad he is my dad.

<u>Read and Recall:</u>

my   is   the   best   am   glad   he
🟢   🟢   🟢   🟢   🟢   🟢   🟢

| ag |

Word Family

ag

Wag The Dog

I see Wag.

He is my dog.

He wags his tail.

He is happy.

Read and Recall:

see he my his is happy tail

| am | Word Family

am
●
Pam and Sam

Pam likes ham.

Sam likes jam.

Pam and Sam eat ham and jam.

Read and Recall:

am likes and eat

an	**Word Family**

an

<u>The Man Dan</u>

The man is Dan.

He is in the van.

Dan has a red hat on his head.

<u>Read and Recall:</u>

the man he in has red head

| ap | Word Family

ap

Sam Has a Red Cap

Sam has a red cap.

He naps with his cap.

His cap has a flap.

Read and Recall:

has   red   naps   his   with   flap

36

| at |

Word Family

at
●

The Fat Cat

The cat is fat.

The cat is on the mat. The cat plays with the rat.

<u>Read and Recall:</u>

the on plays with rat fat

| ed |

Word Family

ed

The Red Bed

Ted has a bed.

The bed is red.

He likes to sleep on his big, red bed.

Read and Recall:

the   has   he   to   on   his   big

| en | Word Family

en

Ben Has a Hen

Ben has a hen.

The hen is red.

The hen is Ren.

Ren lays eggs for Ben.

Read and Recall:

has the lays eggs for

| et |

Word Family

et

My Dad is a Vet

My dad is a vet.

The cat is at the vet.

The cat is my pet.

The cat is not well.

Read and Recall:

my   is   not   well

| ig |

Word Family

ig

Tig The Pig

Tig the pig is big.

He likes to eat figs.

He likes to dig holes.

Tig likes mud.

Read and Recall:

the   big   likes   he   to   mud

in Word Family

in

Jin Has a Pin

Jin has a pin.

The pin is by her fin.

Jin likes to spin with a pin by her fin.

Read and Recall:

has spin her likes with by

| ip | **Word Family**

ip

<u>Zip Me Up</u>

I see a zip.

The zip is blue.

I see a zip.

It is on my shoe.

<u>Read and Recall:</u>

see   me   up   it   my   shoe   blue

it

Word Family

it

Sam Gets Fit

Sam gets fit.

He runs and runs.

Sam likes to run to get fit.

Read and Recall:

gets fit and runs likes

| ob |

Word Family

ob

Bob Has a Job

Bob has a job.

He eats corn on the cob.

He likes to eat corn on the job.

Read and Recall:

has   he   on   corn   the   likes   eat

| og |

Word Family

og

Fred The Dog

Fred the dog is a black dog.

He jumps on the log.

He plays with the frog.

Read and Recall:

the is jumps with he plays

| op | Word Family

op

The Cop

I see a cop.

He likes to hop.

I see a cop at the bus stop. Stop! Stop! Stop!

Read and Recall:

see   likes   he   at   the   bus   stop

| ot | Word Family

ot
The Hot Sun

The sun is hot.

It looks like a big dot.

Read and Recall:

the hot looks big like

| ub |

Word Family

ub

Jen is in The Tub

Jen is in the tub.

She likes to rub her fur.

Jen is my cat.

Read and Recall:

in   the   is   likes   rub   fur   my

| ug | Word Family

ug
Tom Has a Bug

Tom has a bug.

The bug sleeps on the rug.

Tom gives it a hug.

The bug is happy.

Read and Recall:

has   the   bug   on   gives   it   happy

| un |

Word Family

un

Fun in The Sun

Jen had fun in the sun.

The sun is hot.

Jen had a bun and fun in the sun.

Read and Recall:

had   in   the   is   bun   and

| ut |

Word Family

ut

The Rot Nut

I live in a hut.

The door I shut.

I eat a nut.

It hurts my gut.

It was a rot nut.

Read and Recall:

live door shut eat my hurts was

"a" says its own name.

"i" and "y" make no sound

Vowel Digraphs/Teams

ai and ay

Read and Recall:

paint, rain, chain, pain, tail mail, nail

bay, day, ray, lay, pay, may, say, hay

I pr<u>ay</u> for the r<u>ai</u>n to go aw<u>ay</u>. I pr<u>ay</u> for the r<u>ai</u>n to go aw<u>ay</u>, so I can pl<u>ay</u> and dad can p<u>ai</u>nt. Pl<u>ay</u>ing is fun and so is p<u>ai</u>nting.

52

"ea" an "ee" both make the long "e" sound.

Vowel Digraphs/Teams

ea and ee

Read and Recall:

tea, beat, heat, meat, neat, bean

bee, tree, free, sheep, keep, weep

I met a b<u>ee</u>.

I sip my t<u>ea</u>.

I climb a tr<u>ee</u> and <u>ea</u>t some b<u>ea</u>ns. I like to <u>ea</u>t b<u>ea</u>ns with t<u>ea</u> in the tr<u>ee</u>.

o says its own name.

oo is the sound as in moon

Vowel Digraphs/Teams

oa and long oo

Read and Recall:

oat, coat, boat, soap, loaf, goat

moon, spoon, tooth, moo, food, zoo

I see a g<u>oa</u>t in the r<u>oa</u>d.

The m<u>oo</u>n is dull and the g<u>oa</u>t is old.

I can hear a t<u>oa</u>d. I give it some f<u>oo</u>d with a sp<u>oo</u>n.

cr<u>oa</u>k, cr<u>oa</u>k, cr<u>oa</u>k

Vowel Digraph/Team

Short vowel oo

<u>Read and Recall:</u>

wool, book, look, took, cook, hood

My mom is a good cook.

She has a cookbook.

She likes to bake bread and cook from her cookbook.

Diphthongs

ou and ow

Read and Recall:

house, mouse, round, shout, out, about

bow, cow, how, town, now, brown, down

A mouse came inside the house.

It took a bow and ran about.

"Look it there!" I shouted.

The brown cat will catch it.

Diphthongs

oy and oi

Read and Recall:

Roy, toy, boy, joy, soy, annoy, destroy

oil, coin, boil, soil, toil, spoil, noise, voice

Roy has a toy van.
He gives it to a boy for a coin. The boy is happy and so is Roy.

Consonant Digraph

sh sh sh

Read and Recall:

she, share, shell, ship, sheep, shark

lash, cash, fish, dish, rush, lash, rash

Fish in a Dish

Mom sends me to the shop. I can see a ship on the sea. A man sells fish at the shop. He sells fish for cash.

Consonant Digraph

ch ch ch

Read and Recall:

chair, church, chicken, chest, cheek

chin, bench, bunch, chat, lunch, chop

The Church Chair

Mom likes to sit on the church chair, where she can see the chickens. One day she fell off the chair and hurt her chin, cheek and chest.

Consonant Digraph

th th th

Read and Recall:

third, thin, thirty, thumb, three, thank

the, them, their, those, that, they, there

I Won Third Prize

I won third prize in the race. I took the prize from my teacher and said, "thank you."

Consonant Digraph

wh wh wh

Read and Recall:

why, what, when, where, while, who

whether, whale, white, whose, whip

Mr. White

Who is that man? He is my dad. His name is Mr. White. He likes to ride his bike. When he finishes riding his bike, he will whip up a drink.

Consonant Digraph

ph ph ph

Read and Recall:

phone, alphabet, sphere, phase, photo

Phil Likes to Take Photos

Phil likes to take photos with his phone. He takes a photo of himself. He likes to take photos of his friends, Phillip and Sophia.

Consonant Digraph

kn kn kn

<u>Read and Recall:</u>

knee, knot, know, knock, knife, knead

Knox Can Tie a Knot

Knox can tie a knot.
He likes to tie a lot.
He knocks on the door
and falls on one knee.
Mummy! Mummy! I did it.

Consonant <u>Digraph</u>

<u>ck ck ck</u>

<u>Read and Recall:</u>

tick, pick, lick, kick quick, rock, shock

lock, sock, clock, mock, knock, quack

<u>The Clock on The Wall</u>

The clock on the wall is sick. The clock on the wall will not tick. I lock the door and walk outside. The clock begins to tick, tick, tick, tick, tick.

Consonant Digraph

ss ss ss

Read and Recall:

mess, cross, kiss, bless, grass, dress

The Red Dress

Jane likes to wear red. She dresses in her red dress. She is going to a party. Tom makes a mess and soils Jane's dress. Jane begins to cry, what a mess!

Consonant Digraph

ll ll ll

Read and Recall:

bell, sell, tell, well, shell, fell, hell

Jack and Jill (nursery rhyme)

Jack and Ji**ll** went up the hi**ll** to fetch a pail of water. Jack fe**ll** down and broke his crown, and Ji**ll** came tumbling after.

Consonant Digraph

ng ng ng

Read and Recall:

long, hang, sang, song, lungs, wrong

king, sing, ring, wings, stung, strong

The King Sings a Song

The king likes to sing. He sings to the queen.

He asks a bird to help with a song. The bird sings to the top of her lungs.

Beginning Blends

sl and cl

Read and Recall:

slap, slide, slow, sly, slug, slip, slice

clap, clean, climbs, clock, class, clown

Claire Has a Slug

Claire has a slug. It is very slow. Claire climbs up, takes a brick and throws it at the slug. The slug will not go.

Beginning Blends

sl and cl

Slater The Clown

Slater the clown was so slow. He was clumsy and sloppy. He sleeps with a clothes spin on his nose.

Beginning Blends

fl and pl

Read and Recall:

fly, flip, flap, flame, flee, flower

plants, plait, plate, plug, plums, plus

Florence Plants a Flower

Florence plants a flower and waters it every day. She eats plums and plaits her hair. Florence watches her flower grows into a pretty rose.

Beginning Blends
fl and pl

Flora Plaits Her Hair

Flora likes to plait her hair. She flips and plays a lot. Flora plaits her hair then flips and plays.

Beginning Blends

bl and gl

Read and Recall:

blink, blind, black, blue, blood, bloom

glad, glue, glow, glove, glitter, glass

The Blue Glove

I have a blue glove. I put it on my right hand. The glue does not stick to my hand. The blue glove keeps my hand clean.

Beginning Blends

bl and gl

The Blue Glitter Glue

I am glad to have some blue glitter glue in a glass.

The blue glitter glue glows on my gloves.

The gloves keep the glitter off my hands.

Beginning Blends

br and tr

<u>Read and Recall:</u>

brag, brush, bring, brick, brave, brother

truck, try, trade, trim, tree, trick

My Brother Trad

My brother Trad wants to trade his truck for a brush. My name is Brad. Trad likes to trick me, so he can play with my toy truck.

Beginning Blends

br

Brad Likes Bread

Brad likes bread.
He is a bright boy.
Brad uses his brain.
He does his homework and never complains.

Beginning Blends

tr

Travis on a Trip

Travis is on a trip to Trinidad. He gets stuck in traffic. He comes out of his tractor. He sits by some trash.

Beginning Blends

cr and fr

Read and Recall:

cry, crib, crime, crab, crumbs, croaks

fry, friends, frog, free, fruit, Friday

The Frog Wears a Crown

Fred the frog wears a crown. He makes friends with Mr. Crab and eats crumbs in his crib. He croaks and croaks.

Beginning Blends

cr and fr

Creepy The Crab

Creepy the crab crawls out of the crack. He met Freddy the frog jumping from pond to pond. Creepy and Freddy wants to be free.

Beginning Blends
dr and gr

Drizzly The Green Dragon

I see Drizzly the green dragon. Her dress is made of grass. She gives a big grin and dries her hair. She is a pretty dragon.

Beginning Blends

dr and gr

Read and Recall:

drink, drop, dreams, drill, drag, draws

grab, grapes, great, grade, grin, green

Drake Draws Grapes

Drake draws grapes. He likes to drink grape juice. He grabs his brush and paint. He dreams of grapes all the time.

Beginning Blends

sn and st

Read and Recall:

snow, snail, snake, sneeze, snore

stays, start, step, still, store

Snora The Snail

Snora the snail likes to snore. She stays in her shell all day. She is afraid to step out.

She curls up in her shell.

Beginning Blends

sp and sk

Read and Recall:

spider, spit, spin, spoon, spot, spy

sky, skill, skip, skit, skirt, skate

Spot The Spider

Spot the spider has a skill. She likes to spin webs and skip with her friends. She spins and skips, skips, and spins. She is a happy spider.

Ending blend

mp mp mp

Read and Recall:

jump, bump, lamp, stamp, camp, limp

A Letter to Gramp

I need a stamp to send a letter to Gramp. I lit the lamp and stick on a stamp, that I got from the camp. Gramp will be happy to hear from me.

Ending Blend

nk nk nk

Read and Recall:

bank, tank, pink, wink, think, thank

I Drink Some Water

I drink some water to quench my thirst. I think if I drink some more my tummy will burst.

Ending Blend

nd nd nd

Read and Recall:

and, hand, band, grand, land, sand

find, kind, wind, bend, pond, blind

Mom's Band

Mum has a band.
She plays on the land. She dances on the sand. The music is grand.

Ending Blend

nt nt nt

Read and Recall:

ant, bent, dent, sent, tent, want

plant, print, spent, went, hunt, paint

Trent Lives in a Tent

Trent lives in a tent. The tent is bent. Trent eats ants in his bent tent, poor Trent.

R Controlled Vowels
ar, er, ir, or, ur

Beware of Bossy R

AR	ER	IR	OR	UR
car	her	bird	for	hurt
hard	verb	first	more	nurse
far	cover	dirt	store	turtle
start	water	shirt	corn	blur
art	after	third	cord	turkey
farm	hunger	stir	sport	purple
arm	letter	girl	form	fur

88

Now we know the magic e

Read and Recall:

ā
bake, cake, date, fade, gave, hate
lame, name, rate, sake, take, wake

ī
bride, dine, five, fine, hide, kite, nine
ride, rise, site, tide, wise, wide, wipe

ō
bone, coke, dose, hole, hope, home joke,
lone, nose, pose, rope, stone

ū
cube, cute, fuse, fume, huge, June mute,
mule, rule, tune, tube, use

The magic "e (silent e) turns short vowels into long vowels.

| ā | **Magic E short stories**

Long ā

I Hate to be Late

"I hate to be late," said Nate. Nate awakes and bakes a cake. He gives a wave to his mom. He will not be late for school.

| ī | ## Magic E short stories

Long ī

Nike's Bike

Nike likes to ride his bike. He rides his bike to the park. He has a red bike. Nike wipes his bike and keeps it clean.

| ō | **Magic E short stories**

Long ō

The Big Hole

I fell into a big hole.

I broke my leg bone.

I called Jane on the phone.

She sent me a note.

It reads, get well soon.

| ū | **Magic E short stories**

Long ū

Cute June

June is a cute girl.

Cute June likes to play.

She plays one tune on her flute.

Kindergarten Sight Words

my	name	is	I	am
live	in	a	of	at
and	is	play	big	ran
come	it	said	like	what
for	was	see	help	my
we	here	no	yes	blue
yellow	red	brown	black	green
away	make	find	can	little
the	go	look	to	have
me	jump	not	three	two
up	down	where	what	why

Pre-Primer Sight Words

a	find	is	not	three
and	for	it	one	to
away	funny	jump	play	two
big	go	little	red	up
blue	help	look	run	we
can	here	make	said	where
come	I	me	see	yellow
down	in	my	the	you

Primer Sight Words

all	do	no	say	want
am	eat	now	she	was
are	four	on	so	well
at	get	our	soon	went
ate	good	out	that	what
be	have	please	there	white
black	he	pretty	they	who
brown	into	ran	this	will
but	like	ride	too	with
came	must	saw	under	yes

First Grade Sight Words

The 100 Most Frequently Used Words				
a	did	her	over	this
about	do	him	people	three
after	dog	his	play	time
all	down	home	ran	to
an	for	just	said	too
and	from	like	saw	two
are	get	little	school	up
as	go	man	see	us
at	going	me	she	very
back	good	morning	so	was
be	got	mother	some	water
because	I	my	soon	we
big	if	night	started	went
but	in	not	that	were
by	into	of	the	what
call	is	off	their	when
came	it	on	them	will
can	had	one	then	with
could	have	our	there	would
day	he	out	they	you

Segmenting sight words to improve spelling

Words	Segmenting				sounds
up	ŭ	p			2
name	n	ā	m	¢	3
play	p	l	ay		3
blue	b	l	ue		3
have	h	ă	v	¢	3
where	wh	ere			2
yellow	y	ĕ	ll	ow	4
green	g	r	ee	n	4
brown	b	r	ow	n	4
make	m	ā	k	¢	3
saw	s	aw			2
soon	s	oo	n		3
with	w	ĭ	th		3
about	ă	b	ou	t	4
what	wh	ă	t		3

Segmenting sight words to improve spelling

Words	Segmenting				Sounds
can	c	a	n		3
mouse	m	ou	s	¢	3
boy	b	oy			2
yes	y	ĕ	s		3
nose	n	ō	(z) s	¢	3
zoo	z	oo			2
hug	h	ŭ	g		3
net	n	ĕ	t		3
she	sh	ē			2
out	ou	t			2
read	r	ea	d		3
back	b	ă	ck		3
sight	s	ī	t		3
boat	b	oa	t		3
ship	sh	ĭ	p		3

I'm Gonna Love Reading Rif, Rif

Refrain
I'm gonna love reading, rif, rif
I'm gonna love reading, rif, rif
Reading is fun, reading is fun
Reading is fun, rif, rif

Reading helps me to read the questions
Reading helps me to find the answers
Reading helps me to be a leader
Reading helps me as a boredom buster

Reading helps me to use my words well
Reading helps me to be successful
Reading helps me to do my very best
Reading will help me to pass the test

Written by Yvette Gittens

The end

We have come to the end of this pre-primer and primer reader. I trust that the children would have enjoyed all the stories in this edition. I do believe that teachers should take advantage of intentional moments to teach structured literacy in every subject. This approach will definitely help students with learning challenges and has proven to be one of the best approaches for all readers.

Thumbs up to all the parents, teachers, and educators and to our wonderful students who will one day be tomorrow's leaders.

Students must learn to decode and blend with automaticity so that they can read fluently. Students must develop phonological awareness, phonemic awareness, phonics skills along with orthographic mapping so that they form phonemes and graphemes connections which will help them in recalling what they have read.

We can do this:
Let us box the dent out of literacy.

Made in the USA
Columbia, SC
14 November 2024